Writing Prompts
and Helpful Exercises
in 22 Categories

Lisa J Lickel

and David J Rank

Through its programs, the Novel-In-Progress Bookcamp & Writing Retreat strives to provide useful advice and instruction on the writing craft and publishing trends, focused on the book-length writing projects of our clients, in a friendly and encouraging venue. Open to writers of all fiction genres and creative nonfiction.

NOVEL-IN-PROGRESS
BOOKCAMP
& WRITING RETREAT

www.NovelBookCamp.org

Writing Prompts
and Helpful Exercises
in 22 Categories

Fox Ridge Publications

Novel-In-Progress Bookcamp & Writing Retreat, Inc.

Writing Prompts and Helpful Exercises in 22 Categories
© by Lisa J Lickel

First Edition, July 1, 2021
Writing Craft

Novel-In-Progress Bookcamp & Writing Retreat, Inc.
www.novelbookcamp.org

Print ISBN   9798742845201

Cover image by Engin Akyurt from Pixabay

Independently Published by Fox Ridge Publications for
Novel-In-Progress Bookcamp & Writing Retreat, Inc.

Hillsboro, Wisconsin
www.LisaLickel.com

For Phil N. Martin, who probably would have had a lot to say about this project over a nice glass of wine...

fraværende venner

Skoll!

Table of Contents

Fiction

Non-Fiction

Introduction

Most writers hit a bump now and then. Maybe it's not an outright case of writer's block but a minor tantrum that has you stuck staring at a blank concrete wall at the end of a dark alley in blinding rain with *those guys* chasing you...no way out. Or is there?

We recognize there are numerous categories and genres not covered here, such as script writing, graphic novels, short story formats, essay, or spoken/sung word, besides the plethora of sub-genres. Maybe we'll get to those in volume two. These gentle definitions and encouraging prompts and exercises can be twisted to fit your own unique stories. If you need a nudge or a shove, mix and match a prompt from different categories to jumpstart your creativity. Grab a notebook or whatever makes you happy to noodle around and start stirring the soup! Sometimes a walk around the block is every bit as effective as butt in chair.

And, if you really need a jolt, come to Bookcamp. Mingle with writers from all over the US and Canada who've experienced a full week immersion with your work in progress, networking and meeting industry professionals from New York Times best-selling authors, to mid-list ones, to editors, publishers, agents, and everyone in between—all with big dreams—while being well cared for on the grounds of an amazing retreat center in beautiful Wisconsin. You might make some mighty fine friends too. Find details at the end of this book.

Fiction

Fiction is prose in which an author creatively uses imagination to devise a fine story.

Creating Fiction is more than writing make believe, telling lies, or inventing impossible scenarios. In fact, it's the opposite: it's making your reader *believe*. Are you familiar with the idea of "suspend disbelief"? It's an art to spellbind your reader, to keep them turning pages, keep them awake at night, or make them forget to look at their phones for more than ten minutes. Churning out good fiction involves using that temperamental question "what if?" It involves a three-dimensional and deeper study of character and situation. Use our prompts and writing exercises to help turn your story on its head and shake it till the pockets are empty.

Character

Character-driven or story-driven? You've most likely heard that question with a lesson on types of literature or methods of storytelling. Whichever genre you choose, appropriate characterization can drive your story. Everyone is unique. Anyone can "act out of character" at any time and surprise your readers. But even if your people figure out life in or out of character, you need to establish a good base of physical and emotional description, a perceived history to provide relevant action/reaction scenarios, sensible dialog, intimate secrets, agendas, fears, desires, and other yearnings to complicate matters.

- Your character organizes the closet or cleans the car. What do they keep, what do they toss?

- While standing in line casually observe another person. Make a mental image of hair, clothing style, and posture. Make calculated guesses about the person's occupation. Later, jot a list of observed characteristics and create a personality profile which includes imagined profession and personality for a character.

- Have your character pack for a week-long train trip. Then for a weekend camp out. What do they bring and why?

- While returning to his seat after intermission at his daughter's dance recital, your character overhears another couple discussing the performance, specifically mentioning his daughter. What does your character do?

- Your character receives a letter from a former spouse dated five years earlier. Reaction? What does it say?

- What happens in your character's nightmare?

- "I hate my name." Why? What does he/she want to be called?

- What is the last thing your character wanted to learn to do? For what purpose?

- When was the last time your character spoke to a parent? Why?

- "There goes my phone!" Reaction?

- The test was positive. Reaction?

- "Does anyone speak English? My driver stranded me here." Reaction?

- What does your character do for his or her birthday?

Description

Sharing description comes from bias. How you observe and, in turn, tell another what you saw is one of the most expository methods you can use to show readers and involve them in everything about your story. How characters interpret situations, what they think about their setting or circumstances and who they share it with can create defining moments of rising and falling action.

- Look out of the nearest window. List ten things you see. Create a paragraph of at least five sentences using each of the items on your list.

- Close your eyes and count to thirty. With your eyes closed, listen, sniff, and reach out until your fingers contact something. Open your eyes when you have identified some aspect of each sense. Step outside and do the same thing. Make notes of your experience. What surprised you?

- Write a paragraph about your favorite scent.

- Sit in front of a shelf or a cupboard at home and write down everything you notice. Give yourself as much time as you need.

- Watch a travelogue about a place you've never been or look at pictures with someone who's traveled to a place you've never been. Write notes about what you see and experience from how the place is described by the other person.

Dialog

"Through-speak": from Latin and Greek origins, dialog is language shared among people. (monologue: one speaker) Although we tend to think of communicating through spoken and heard recognizable words, consider this data from a 2020 *Lifesize* article: 70-93 percent of language is nonverbal. You've probably heard about "body language"— how gestures, posture, facial expressions, and eye contact communicate more than words. Consider also the rich nuances of sign language and other methods of getting your message across. Interpreting (and misinterpreting) messages creates a complex set of circumstances with which to tell story. Balance natural speech with action beats and avoid wooden delivery or information dumps. Listen carefully to those around you, as well as to yourself. Observe, write conversations verbatim for practice, read your dialog out loud to get a sense of rhythm and mannerisms.

- Turn on a five-minute speech online. TED-Ed talks, www.ted.com, is one great place to find speeches. Listen with the sound off. Note the speaker's facial expression and other gestures. Write a paragraph about what you think the person is saying. Then, replay the same speech with the sound on. Besides analyzing your guess at the speech, pay attention to the inflection of the speaker's voice and have your character practice speaking with different tonal qualities.

- A telephone conversation takes place in which your observing character can hear only one side. What conclusions does your character make? Write it out. Now, switch sides of the conversation.

- Invite your character to a game of Bridge. How does your character play? Competitive? Timid? Aggressive? Skilled or unsure? Good winner or poor loser?

- Two businesspeople from different countries who don't speak the same language meet to arrange a corporate merger over lunch. How do they communicate?

- A child overhears a conversation between adults and makes assumptions. What are they? How does the child react?

- Your character calls customer service and has a difficult time understanding the representative. Why?

- The interviewer leans back in his chair and holds his hands up to his lips like a prayer while you are talking about your past job experience. How does your character interpret this action?

- Your neighbor's five-year-old grandson visiting from Poland rings your doorbell and hands you a bouquet he picked of your prized dahlias from your garden. What do you say?

Fantasy

As a genre, Fantasy literature has unique players that look and act in accepted manners across culture and trope. Trolls, elves, fairies, goblins, dwarves, naiads and dryads, wizards, giants, dragons, unicorns, spells, and the like must be recognizable...but that doesn't mean boring predictability. These wondrous creatures have every bit as much right to act in or out of character as anyone else. Their world can go just as wonky—even more so! Throw together magic, otherworldly creatures, maybe add a couple of confused or obfuscating humans, toss up some goals, pitch a wicked bunch of conflicts and watch the scales fly.

- A goblin and a troll buy adjoining property and build their own homes. One of them gets a dog. What happens next?

- The dragon must choose a successor and share the secret of the hidden treasure before it dies.

- All of the spells perform half of their intent.

- The unicorn was not supposed to enter the portal unaccompanied.

- The naiad began to choke as her gills grew closed.

- What are the rules of magic?

- Describe the setting for your story. Mountains, jungle, islands?

- What does your villain want? What does the villain need?

Horror

That moment when the hair rises on the back of your neck. The feeling someone is watching you through the closed curtain. An icepick. Wisps of mist, a touch from someone who's not there. The lump in your throat, the extra-quick trot of your heartbeat. The impossible change happening in front of you. The desperate need to get out...to scream, to run but you can't move. Yeah, that's horror. Bigger than mystery and often gorier than thrillers, there's that rising sense of peril and panic that must be answered and thwarted, but probably won't happen, even when you're sure you stopped the bad guy.

- A trail of blood ends at the bedroom wall. How does your main character react?

- The phone rang and rang. Kelly put his hands over his ears as he stared at the bare wires where his parents' harvest gold trimline used to hang.

- That itchy spot on her skin grew spiky orange hairs.

- Jimmy returns from two weeks at camp. You catch him outside at midnight. You don't need a flashlight to see that he's eating dirt in the flowerbeds because...

- You wake up and put on your new glasses. You blink at the sight of a woman you've never seen before sitting on the edge of the bed. She doesn't respond to your question and no way are you reaching out to touch her. When you take the glasses off, she's not there. When you put them back on, she...

-

- A new home, a fresh start. It's high noon and a sunny day. Yet you feel uneasy. Something is wrong. What is it?

- You're hiking a trail deep in a national park and you realize something is following you. What do you do?

- While rooting in your basement for that box, a spider drops from its web in front of you and offers you two wishes. What do you choose?

- You take your dog out at night in your new neighborhood and notice an unusual amount of firefly activity in the bushes between your house and the neighbor you haven't met. Do you investigate?

- You check on little Jimmy before going to bed. You notice someone sitting in the rocking chair. Who or what is it?

- Even when Rory was alive, he would never have done...

- The headline on the newspaper is all about the anniversary of your unsolved, gruesome murder...dated next year.

- In your quarters on the space ship, , there's something wrong with your lavatory mirror. Until you can call maintenance, you finally throw and towel over it to hide the reflection of the thing that's definitely not *you*.

Literary

The melding pot or the aegis of genre, literary writing as its own style can be confusing and gets a bad rep from readers or bookshelvers who don't know what to do with it. Think issue-driven, dramatic, often tragic, book club books where characters struggle against insurmountable odds with plenty of soul searching, which they sometimes can't overcome. It's a huge category mostly because it can't be defined in a nutshell. Readers will start to describe the book, "It's about..." and then scratch their heads. Many writers are desperate to write the next big seller, the next major prize winner, to be recognized by the critics (and often puzzle readers), and optioned for a major motion picture. This is that category.

- Create five no-win situations. How would your character approach each of them?

- Create a family tree of at least three generations. Give them a medical concern they pass down.

- "In this court, you're guilty until proven innocent." What is the crime?

- "If I hadn't done it, someone else would have. I did it for you, so you could be happy." Does "it" make your character happy?

- Find an obituary and devise three plot points based on the deceased's recorded highlights.

- What is your main character's occupation? Why is he or she unsatisfied with it?

- Is your character single, married, or divorced? Why is he or she unhappy with her situation?

- What does your main character prize the most? House, car, family heirloom, past accomplishment?

- What could make your main character happy? Why can't he or she achieve it?

- Who would play the movie version of your characters and why?

- Where and when does your story take place? What major event defines the moment and echoes into the future?

- Think about why this story is not a mystery (see page 15), or a romance (see page 16) and jot down notes about what would have to happen in your story to fit it into one of those categories, and why you're not doing that.

- What childhood fantasy did your character have that never materialized? How does it affect his or her choices?

- Who would your character tell his or her deepest secret?

Mystery

Genre has certain criteria, otherwise it would be something else. Readers may not always be able to say what makes the book a mystery or a romance or a western using author-speak, but they know what they expect. A mystery may be unraveling the source of a crime or answering questions, or a combination. A mystery is some event that initially appears inexplicable, and a person or team of people search for clues that lead to the solution. Similar genres include Thrillers and Crime stories, Procedurals, and sub-categories such as Cozy Mysteries. These all have slightly different elements, but all involve a process to deconstruct a puzzling situation.

- Your character opens the refrigerator. It's empty.

- A car accident occurs in front of your character's home. He goes inside to call in a report. When the authorities arrive, there is no sign of an accident.

- The end of the text is cut off. Which street has a house number 4167? Time is running out.

- A fish caught and cleaned has a key in its gut.

- You arrange a lunch date and tour with your new neighbor who just moved in last week. When you go to pick her up, she's not there, nor does the house appear to have had an occupant in the last six months.

Romance

Like all genre literature, romance has many sub-categories. Certain typical plot points, rising and falling action, the moment the lovers meet, conflicts, the conclusion, are all expected aspects of romantic literature. But like every story, how you spin those expected moments, the baggage you give your characters, the spoilers they must survive, and the choices they make to satisfy their deepest longings, even sacrificial choices, are what keep romance readers happy. Readers want to see those odds overcome to make that happily-ever-after ending. It's the best-selling book category in all its variety of flavors. What's romantic about the following situations?

- The check arrives, only it's not the amount promised.

- The best man can't find the ring and stops the wedding.

- An elderly neighbor your character knew all his or her life is stunningly being deported.

- A judge declines to hear the case.

- On my first visit to Palazzo Ducale, I backed into an artwork. Bas Relief—impasto. Oil. Fresh.

- Your best friend talks you into going on an exotic vacation with her, then strands you alone at the resort. What do you do?

Science Fiction

Science Fiction literature employs a sense of adventure, probable discovery, and use of realistic inventions. It is literature that explores possible interaction and interference with our world and our universe through natural law. Science can catch up to imagination, so think far abroad. Science fiction covers a fairly wide range of illusion including time travel, space travel, life in futuristic societies or societies on other worlds, association or war or misunderstanding with other-worldly beings, inventions and power sources that do not yet exist (for your audience, yet) but make life easier or more difficult for your characters. They are often survival stories. While the genre is fiction, there are physical laws that still must be obeyed, whether in the known world or an invented universe. Issues that come up or problems are solved or explained with recognizable science, not magic, even if the culture where they're used doesn't have the knowledge base to recognize them as (human) invention.

- On an extraterrestrial diplomatic mission, your character must choose between a potentially toxic and a safe meal to eat to prove trustworthiness.

- A mistranslation of "weapons" and "equipment" causes an inappropriate shipment of goods.

- The colonists have run out of supplies from home and must begin eating native flora and/or fauna.

- Describe a world where bacteria is the dominant species.

- You are part of an advance scout team exploring the galaxy for the next outpost. You've done reconnaissance all day. In the morning, you exit your ship and see a footprint that wasn't there yesterday.

- If you snip this code here...like this, see? And insert this piece here, like so...and add a little bit from here...see? See what happens? Oh, wait...I meant...oh, wow...

- Describe a non-human who breathes carbon dioxide.

- Robots—friends or enemies of humankind?

- What new technology revolutionizes life on Earth?

- People find it easier to live in a virtual world rather than reality. What happens next?

- There's a bomb under a bench in the middle of a crowded festival on the neutral recreation planet Etude.

- Your friend who grew up in the colony on Ganymede is visiting Earth for the first time and sets out to prove the mathematical possibility of how bumblebees fly.

- All of the food on this planet turns gray when it's processed. This is your first visit and you don't know what you're eating. What do you do?

Setting

The situation in which you place your characters should make a difference to the story. Can your story happen any other place, under any other circumstances? In any time frame, anywhere on (or off) this world? Setting involves place (geography, interior/exterior) and time frame (era, season, day/night). These criteria will affect how your people act and react, how they speak, dress, eat, sleep, travel, and comport themselves. In some stories, the setting can play an integral role.

- Go for a walk outdoors or around your current space and note the first two colors you see. Where else in your short walk do you find those colors? When you return to your writing, quickly write down everything you saw with those two colors.

- When your character encounters "winter," how does he or she react?

- Describe entering and walking around an empty house using all of your senses.

- Find a historical weather data website and look up an unusual weather event in or near your book's setting or likely fictional setting. How might a significant event affect the current setting?

- Pluck a scene from your book and put it at an airport or in a hotel.

Youth

Literature for high school and younger readers has grown and split into a variety of sub-genres for target audiences in recent decades. Juvenile, Young Adult, Early Reader, Middle Grade, Picture, Children's Literature, New Adult, Chap books make up some of the categories. They overlap, and to make it more confusing, librarians and booksellers can choose a category to shelve a book. Picture books use very few words, but words chosen are crucial. Early Reader and Middle Grade are graded for readability and appropriate age reader based on vocabulary and sentence structure tests. They feature characters about three years older than their target audience. Serious writers of juvenile fiction choose single themes, know their audience, and understand grade-appropriate vocabulary. Literature for younger readers can successfully be every bit as plot-involved or creative as literature for adults. Who will read your book?

- Choose a favorite adult book and write a synopsis of it using vocabulary suitable for third graders.

- Create a one-page biography for a child who might have lived in your neighborhood fifty years in the past or fifty years in the future.

- Flip a bullying situation on its head.

- A child with learning issues wants to cook a meal.

- Your twelve-year-old character's best friend has a secret.

- What prompts a desire to run away?

- Create an "exploring kit" first from the point of view of a child character, then from the point of view of the adult in the child character's life.

- Take your character horseback riding.

- Start a community project, such as a garden or a summer reading program.

- Mom dropped me off at the wrong summer camp!

- "I'm allergic."

- Your character needs glasses.

- He's desperate to join the guys at the water hole but doesn't swim.

- The au pair has an emergency.

- "Ew! You have six toes!"

- "Why do you get to change in the bathroom instead of here with us in the locker room?"

- Ever since she saw that movie, she's been afraid of water, even drinking it or taking a bath, or...you know. How can your character help her friend overcome a fear like this?

Beginnings

Where do you start your story? At the beginning, of course. That's trickier than it sounds. What is your story about? What are the goals and the traps? What does your character need desperately, or think he needs, that he's willing to do anything to get it? Bake up an unforgettable aha-moment first line. Set the table for your reader. At first glance we wonder if we're getting lobster or a cheeseburger. Readers should be able to sniff the cooking aroma and hear the clattering pots in the kitchen. Authors should get out the way and allow to the series of unfortunate events unfold in progress.

- The car's front passenger wheels graze the edge of the road.

- An envelope that color could bear no good news.

- Was it the crack of the bat or the crack of the ball hitting...

- Only nitwits get lost in the neighborhood where they grew up.

- My palazzo pants were obviously wrong for this party.

- Emergency vehicles stop outside your house in the middle of the night, waking you up.

- In a crowded room your character sees...

- In a sentence, show your reader something about what your character wants.

Middles

You have an explosive opening and a dynamite ending...and 200-300 pages in between. If you're a pantser, ow. If you're a plotter, you probably don't need these prompts. Many authors use this part of the book to justify their wildest dreams. When things are starting to go well, throw a wrench in the works, hurt someone, start a fire, steal a horse, drop something down a well. Conflict—creative and organic conflict—gives rise to the tension on which you coil your story. You've set up the goal—that desired object or circumstance that your character will die without—so here's your chance to show everyone why your characters cannot possibly achieve their goals no matter how hard they try, or who they pester to help them. The realm of possibility, the kingdom of suspended disbelief, has wide borders and cunning defenders. Stay alert.

- The diagnosis didn't confirm food poisoning.

- At Wendell's funeral, my sister Jan laughed.

- Foreclosure was coming.

- The designer dress I was to wear down the runway, the one that fit perfectly last week,...

- "Yeah, I'm calling about your loser loner car."

- New information is found. Does it help or hinder?

- Throw that crummy goldfish and his bowl off the roof.

Ends

All good things must find a satisfactory denouement. Every genre has a goal to reach and it's your authorial honor to guide your reader toward that goal while not yanking their chains or feeding it to them with a silver spoon. Even serials must reach a point when the main goal is achieved no matter what the character's original desire, even if there are a couple of dangling threads for a sequel. A book should conclude in an appropriate way for the main storyline, or it's called something else—usually not nice things by your reader who does not care to be left dangling over a cliff if they're not anticipating it. Those chapter serials in magazine and websites and newspapers are different. Readers expect it, and they have a subscription and a promised next chapter. Certain genres have expected endings: romance is happily ever after even if it's messy; westerns go riding off into the sunset, even if it's just for a picnic; mysteries get solved; horror often involves severed parts and the promise of not being over; the dragon gets the gold in fantasy; thrillers involve surviving danger; memoir reaches the next stage; journalism concludes with a result.

- The operation was not successful.

- Your character signs the paper.

- The love interest doesn't show for the wedding.

- A shovel clinks against something hard.

- The ashes blow back in your face.

Nonfiction

Nonfiction uses authenticated events, people, and documented, verified facts to share information typically in article or book form. You may ask why poetry is nonfiction. You're asking the wrong person.

Building Nonfiction is more than putting a series of facts together. It's perspective, it's analysis, and it's an important record for the benefit of others who may not be directly involved in the event or know the people involved but desire the information. We want to engage our readers in our memories, our choices, our careers, and our opinions to create a bond. We want to bring our readers into our communal recollection, to welcome them and make them feel a part of our story and encourage them to share it with others. And that's the goal of every writer, whether fiction or nonfiction. The prompts and exercises in this section are both practical and whimsical, easily bridging fiction and nonfiction.

Use the tools of non-fiction to enhance your storytelling.

Back cover description

The back cover or inside fly leaf of a book, AKA the "blurb," competes with the cover for book browsers. After checking title and author recognition, many potential readers turn the book over to read the back, or open the flap, before they check the contents or read the first page. Every reader has a different approach to choose a book. Entice your readers. Inspire them. Give them a reason to choose you. What will the reader experience when they read your book? What can they expect? Why must they read it?

- If someone asks you "What is your book about?" what would you say? Write it out and practice delivering your response. Pare the description down to 300 words. Then pare it down to 200 words.

- Pick out three things that make your story unique. Write a sentence or two using those terms.

- How will your reader's life change because of your book?

- Who do you picture reading your book? Where and under what circumstances?

- What burning question does your story answer?

- Identify your book's purpose and category.

Creative Non-fiction

Say you have 20-20 hindsight, or could watch the results of an audio-video recording from a device planted at the scene of the event you want to write about. But you don't. You know the facts—when the *Titanic* sank, and the crew and passenger manifest—but you don't know word-for-word the conversation in the galley. You want to write the story of the chefs and kitchen staff. You might have the menus and recipes, but you weren't there to watch how the pastry chef created the pie crusts or which knives the sous chef preferred. You might even have a diary or journal, but you couldn't hear what and how it was being said, or not said. What do you do? Creative non-fiction is more than making things up to fill in the blanks. It's extrapolating from personal papers and interviews, art, interviews. Memories can be faulty; directorial board minutes record results but not how they arrived at the decision. Police reports state when the person of interest was brought in for questioning, but not why they decided to arrest that particular person. Creative non-fiction is going to be filled with your biases; you can't help it, but Creative non-fiction should be based on evidence and the truth as everyone involved understood it. Write Creative non-fiction using all your best literary efforts with goals, angst, appropriate dialog, clippings from reports of the day if you wish, character arc, and denouement. Like all nonfiction, Creative Non-fiction will test your research chops.

- Write down everything you remember from your last vacation or overnight trip away from home.

- What routine household chores do you perform regularly, and how do you do them?

- Describe the last wedding and funeral you attended.

- When considering your topic, draw a vertical line on a page. List the known truths on one side; on the other, jot notes about the creative aspects you'll need to add and how to find them.

- Pick up the nearest newspaper or listen to a newscast and pick a topic of interest. Write a paragraph about your interest in the topic. Then write a paragraph from the opposite point of view—what makes the topic uninteresting or unappealing? How will you turn that around to entice and intrigue your reader?

- Think about high school. Quickly write down the first memory that comes to mind. Dwell on it. Who else was there? What did those people look like? What were they wearing? What were their pet phrases and actions? What dialog do you recall? Now write down what they could have worn or said or done. Use a similar technique in your work.

- Do you know what your grandmother's favorite book was? Your mother's favorite song? Your grandfather's hobby? Your father's childhood pet? Think about what they might have been if you don't know.

- What do you recall about where you were and what you were doing, or how you learned about September 11, 2001. What was your reaction? The reaction of those around you?

History (Research)

Research will always be crucial no matter your topic or subject. History is five minutes, an hour ago; yesterday, an eon ago. Always use a variety of primary, secondary, and tertiary sources to gather information and fact check with more than one resource. Personal interview followed up by confirming details through other observers or analysts of documented records is an example of primary sources— go to the source of information you seek. Reading about the event or person or discovery is an example of secondary information, and tertiary sources are those who are analyzing material that has been gathered by a different party. Use factual, verified information to add believable detail that enhances, not bogs down story no matter what you write.

- Who is the most famous person to come from your community? Find at least one unique detail and write a paragraph about it.

- Locate detailed times of sunrise and sunset (or phase of the moon or eclipse) in your setting. Adjust for daylight savings, and find an appropriate place to use the information in your work.

- Look up the newspapers that were in circulations in your community 100 years ago. Compare to today.

- What slang or idioms do your characters use? How might that be a source of confusion to a character from another part of the country or another era?

- The governing authority issues an edict. What is it and how do your people respond?

- Walk through a cemetery, respectfully, noting the information on the epitaphs, and the style of the tombstones. What stands out to you? What can you tell about people who are buried there?

- Jot down ways communication has changed in your lifetime. Then look up the date each new method was introduced to society. Then cross-reference when these same methods were introduced to countries on at least two other different continents. How will communication affect your characters?

- Do your characters prefer physical books, audio books, digital books, or watching the movie?

- How will your character choose his or her weapon?

- What kind of education did your character receive and where? How does it affect his or her choices and actions?

- What are ten things your readers need to know about the story setting? How will you incorporate them?

- How would your character record or otherwise remember an important event? What tools or devices would be available and how would they choose which to use?

Introduction/Preface/Foreword

Opening material guides the reader into the experience of your book. Authors may write introductory material or a preface, but a foreword is always written by someone other than the author who is familiar with the subject of the book. The front matter gives the author a chance to include information that isn't in the narrative. An *introduction* answers what you want your readers to look for, what they can expect, to take away from your book. A *preface* helps your reader understand why you wrote the book and how you decided to write it. If desired, someone who is an expert in the field of your book's theme, or knowledgeable about the topic, might write additional material for a *foreword* that gives your work added credence.

In fiction, some authors might include prologues and/or epilogues. A *prologue* is material that cannot be included in the narrative of the book either because it happens in a different time frame or place, or to characters not part of the story. If the material you need to share could happen as part of your narrative, then it's chapter one. Prologues should be crucial to the story line, a stage setting tool to help the reader make sense of what they will experience but wouldn't have been something your current characters would have done in the lifetime or the place where your story begins. An *epilogue* might provide additional material to wrap up the prologue or offer a conclusion to the story that takes place in another time frame or setting.

- Write exactly one page about your motives for writing your book.

- If you could choose anyone to write a foreword for your book, who would it be and why?

- Pick a one-word theme that describes your work. How can you use that theme as the focus of your book?

- If your computer ate the first page/scene/chapter of your work, and your notes, what would you do?

- What three things do you, the author, need to know about your material that the reader doesn't need to know?

- What do you hope your readers will know after reading your book?

- Does your book have a call to action? Have you offered advice to help your readers respond to the call?

- Have you used any unusual methods in writing your book, such as interviewing someone famous or traveling to a unique location or searching unusual resources? Mention them and how they helped.

- Is there opening or ending information that you want to share with your reader that is not part of your narrative but an important part of your story? What are the best ways to share that? Consider linking your readers to a separate website landing page or other resource site.

Journalism

Reporting on events for public information is one of the most crucial elements of society. Facts, truth, reality—yes, yes, yes...but. Everyone who participates in, observes first-hand, or interviews someone after the fact (or prior or during), will have a unique perspective. We all come with an individual bias that affects how we, in turn, divulge the information. Journalistic devices in the form of research, being present, interview, fact checking, and distillation of timelines; of the powers of observation, and the ability to add appropriate detail and description that engage the reader are invaluable tools in any writer's kit.

- What five questions would you want to be asked about your book?

- Choose a newspaper or magazine/web article on a topic of interest to you or your character and rewrite it in your or your character's own words.

- Fact-check something you've read recently. What three things do you or your characters find suspicious?

- Create an event for your book launch or some public event in your story. How would the event be publicized?

- Attend or have your character attend a meeting of any kind—local school board, council, PTO, town, civic group. What topics inspire you or your character to take action? Maybe start a letter-writing campaign, circle a petition, or the like?

Memoir

Writing Memoir can also be very helpful for creating or devising a background for a fictional character or for setting development, besides recording a piece of your life for posterity. Memoir differs from Biography or Autobiography in that it singles out an event, a period of time, or series of life choices that lead to a specific event or time frame, such a parenting a special-needs child, a career, a trauma. Biography is a person's life story told by another. Memoir and biographical writing can help promote authentic character development, besides being a cathartic outlet. Everyone has a story, and it's the only thing you take with you when you leave. Share it while you can.

- Choose one of your grade school years. Free write everything you can recall off the top of your head about your teacher, staff, classmates, and the building. If you kept any papers or report cards, yearbooks, newsletters, or other memorabilia from that time of your life, search for it and verify your memories after you've written.

- Think about your least favorite job. Write down everything you recall, from how you decided to apply for the job, the interview if any, your perceived and actual duties, co-workers and anything else you can remember.

- Recall your first, or first memorable date. What do you remember about it? Jot down recollections.

- What do you want your epitaph to reveal about you?

- What is the biggest achievement of your life to date? Write a letter of advice to someone about how you made it happen.

- Write down two or more stories that have been passed down in your family or your favorite fictional family.

- If you knew your grandparents, think about what they were like. Can you separate your childhood memories from memories at different times? If they passed and you attended a funeral, what do you recall about it? Were there lots of people? Was it terribly sad and poignant or a time of happy memories?

- Have you or anyone in your circle been in the armed services? What was that like?

- If you have children or a favorite child in your life, describe him or her. What do you know about them? What do you want to know more about?

- If you could be anything when you grow up, what would it be?

- Are you working in the career of your dreams? Why or why not?

- What do you wish you were brave enough to do?

Poetry

Poetry is the essence of language. It's distillation of thought, both intimate and meant to be shared. It takes many forms, from rhyming couplet to sonnet and everything in between. It can consist of a variety of patterns in sound, form, and subject; syllable counts, running themes, or any number of other rules which may or may not be altered. It is a plea, a prayer, a song, a revelation, or a mystery. It is our sincerest breath. It is very good practice for fiction writers to learn to rid themselves of wordiness or to share a character's essence. Refresh your memory of different types of poetry with https://bookriot.com/different-types-of-poems/ or https://examples.yourdictionary.com/types-of-poetry-examples.html

- Quickly jot 5 haikus about your immediate surroundings.

- Lift a scene from your work in progress and distill it into a rhyming Cinquain.

- If your hero wrote 14 lines of 10 syllables each (aka a sonnet) to prove his worth, what five qualities would he choose?

- What four-line refrain would sum up your character's direst situation?

- Have your main characters describe each other using five senses in an ode.

Web Content

Why should writers care about web content? Unless you're writing under a completely assumed identity, even if you hire out all of your social media or website design and content, or author profiles, you should at least be familiar with and provide guidance to describe your author platform, which includes a short biography and elements of your life that help create a bond with your audience. Writers aren't just selling merchandise, they're selling a recognizable brand, and people want to know what they're buying. What can you share that makes you, or this authorial aspect of you, personal and approachable, either on your own site or on commercial or group sites where readers may find out more about you? What supporting material can you include that helps promote you and your work?

- Write your bio in 200, 100, and 50 words. Focus on your writing and include at least one unique fact.

- Create a 50-word teaser about your book suitable for posting on social media. Include a quote.

- Write a 500-word article about the main theme of your book. Include two or three supporting research sites or resources.

- Write two or three calls for action. What do you want your writer to do after reading your book? How can you quantify any results?

- Write and post a review of a book in a similar genre to yours.

About Novel-In-Progress Bookcamp & Writing Retreat, Inc.

Helping Writers achieve their goals since 2014

www.NovelBookCamp.org

Novel-In-Progress Bookcamp & Writing Retreat offers two intense, 6-day, full-immersion residential writing programs, a novel-writing workshop, and a working writer's retreat typically held in late May annually at a lovely retreat center in Southeast Wisconsin. The concurrent Writing Retreat is designed to provide authors with an alternative for maximum personal time to write, edit, or develop your work-in-progress while surrounded by supportive pros and fellow writers. You have the opportunity to participate in various writing- or publishing-related activities that the general camp offers, should you wish.

The Bookcamp offers morning instruction, an afternoon editing clinic, group critique sessions, discussions on the current publishing industry, one-on-one consultations with our staff, pitch sessions with literary agents and acquisition editors, and presentations on writing or publishing topics.

Writers in all genres working on a novel or creative non-fiction book committed to advancing their writing skills or career goals are eligible to enroll in either of these intensive programs. Check out the available genre camps, as well as all-genre general writers camp. One enrollment fee covers program costs, overnight accommodations, and all meals. Commuter program fees, as well as companion fees are also available depending on space.

Email for more information: director@novelbookcamp.org.
The Bookcamp and Writing Retreat are owned by the Novel-In-Progress Bookcamp & Writing Retreat, Inc., a 501(c)(3) educational nonprofit corporation registered in the State of Wisconsin.